Words from

Another Life

I0428390

By
Deborah D. Johnson

Published by Aubey, LLC in May 2015
Washington, DC
Contains contents of "Words from a Life" and new
writings

www.aubeyllc.com

Designed by Deborah D. Johnson

Table of Contents

Peace

Where do you find it?

If it's not in your home,

Where is it?

If it's not with your spouse and children,
Where is it?

If it's not in your career, job or occupation,
Where is it?

Where is it?

If it's not even with your friends...

Peace is not in any place

or in anyone else.

If peace is not within you,
It's not anywhere.

What's Poetry, Really?

What's poetry?
Some say anyone can write poetry.

If anyone can write poetry

Then...

Anyone can sing an opera,
Anyone can dance a ballet,
Anyone can bake a soufflé,
Anyone can make gravy,
Anyone can transplant a kidney.

Poetry is life.
Poetry comes from a creative heart.
Poetry comes from the spirit.
Poetry comes from dreams.
True poetry touches troubled souls.
It can warm, soothe, heal, or hurt.

A poet is a brave soul with the heart to put life to paper
Then share this with others.

It takes a special person to write poetry.

Family Ties

Strong or
Weak or
Nonexistent.

Helpful or
Encouraging or
Destructive

Family is where
We can find
Love
Hate or
Indifference

My mother's family
Is all of the above.

I pick out the parts that work...

And dump the parts that are

Too painful to think about.

I stand on the encouragement,
Hold to the strong ties,
Believe in the love...where it is.

I know it's there
Sometimes gets covered up a bit
With dust, and gunk and memories.

My Brother at 60

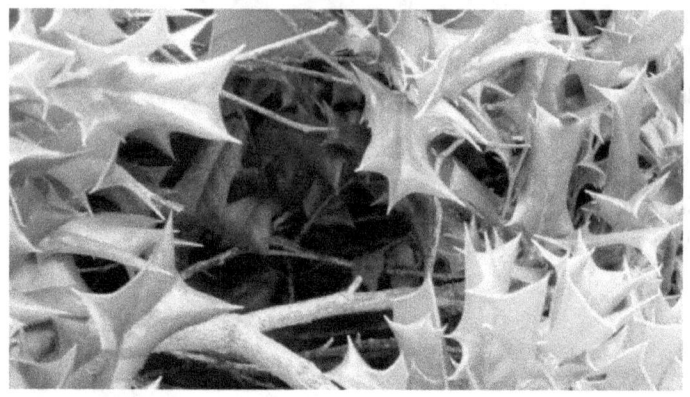

Tall
Strong
Gentle

Always listening;
Really hearing me,
His sister.

Laughs loud still but less often
Smiles now and then
At peace in himself and his family

My brother loves strong.
Works hard.
Helps where he can.

My brother
Is a strong Black man.

Hospitals for Women: Where are they now?

My mother told me I was born in the Columbia Hospital for
Women in the Nation's Capital. My children were born
there. Columbia Hospital for Women will always have a
special place in my heart. It doesn't exist anymore.

That's where I learned to take care of my babies. That's
where I learned to breast feed, even though I chose not to.
That's where a kind and attentive doctor and nursing staff
watched over me, gently moving through labor pains to
birth. Bringing new life into our home.

This was where a nurse sat with me late into the night when
I was crying and lonely during my second hospital stay. I
couldn't go home until my temperature stabilized, and it
wasn't stable.

Columbia Hospital for Women was a place where those of us who needed special attention could get it. Women's bodies are so special and unique. We carry babies and give birth. We go through years and years of menopause. We need checkups and exams for so many things every year or more often depending on our circumstances and health.

Men are special too but...

Women are extra special because God made us with an extra-special purpose.

I miss Columbia Hospital for Women.
It was a special place.

Celebrate Regular People

Some consider regular people less important

than financial institutions.

Some consider regular people less important
than retail chains.

Some even consider regular people less important...

than money.

We work in and for all of these.

We make businesses thrive.

We buy stuff everywhere, every day.

We are more important than –

Money

Influence and
Power

Without us there would be no world.

My Best Friend

My BF is in trouble.
How Do I help?

My BF doesn't want it.
How Do I help?

No one is listening to me.
How do I help?

How can I help?
I can't.
If my BF doesn't want it.

So...

I ask God for help.
I know He can do it.

Are Black People Equal…Now?

I ponder this question. Have Black people finally "arrived"? Do we now go where we want, do what we want (whatever is legal), work where we want, live where we want? Do we receive equal protection under the law? Are we welcomed at all restaurants and vacation resorts?

Are we really:

> given the benefit of the doubt?
> innocent until proven guilty?
> paid fairly for our good work?
> provided standard quality education?
> honored for our contributions to society?

Are we well-represented on executive boards? Do we really have fair and appropriate representation in Congress or on the Supreme Court?

Why do I still have these questions? Still now after the Nation's first Black President won re-election. Why do I still have these questions? Because I see inequalities every day - on television, in neighborhoods, at meetings and conferences, on technical and economic advisory organizations and commissions.

Why in this time in America?

I don't know. Prejudice is a simple word. Prejudice should be easy to identify and erase. But it really isn't.

I just know that there is still a need for a lot of attention to this matter by all of us. Black people aren't "there" yet. I may be convinced if we have another Black president sometime in my life. I might be convinced when the disappearance or death of a Black child engenders extreme outrage, nation-wide attention and heartfelt sympathy.

I would be even more convinced when law officers say that they will leave no stone unturned in finding this missing child or capturing and bringing the murderer to justice, as long as it takes, even if it takes years. So it never happens again; even the Black-on-Black crimes.

But who am I?

Why is my opinion important?

I'm just another Black person...

Conversation with a Black Son
(As a teenager)

I told
you
many
times
that life
is not
fair.
There
are
those
who will
fear you.
There are those who won't like you because you are Black.
There are times you will be treated poorly almost
everywhere you go
Except if you choose to go to prison, of course.

So...
Be careful
Be aware
Pray...a lot

Many have travelled this road before you and thrived.
You must be strong in mind, body and spirit.
You have to show the world who you are and who you will
become.

A strong Black man.

Responsible for yourself and your family.
Proud, successful, God-fearing.

My son,
Stay on the straight and narrow path, no matter what.
Your father did it and still now serves as your strong example.
I know you can do this.

God will guide your way.

We pray every day that He keeps you safe.

Conversation with a Black Daughter
(As a teenager)

No, you
cannot
wear
skin
tight,
short
skirts.
No, you
cannot

wear too short, shorts.
I don't care what everyone else is wearing
You won't.

You don't' need to show so much body.
You are not your body.
You have a strong mind and spirit
You are creative, talented, intelligent.

Don't let others put you down because you choose
to be different.
Don't let others put you down because you are Black.

Honor God and follow His word.

Don't give away your body or your soul.
Know that you are precious.

Use your mind.

Follow your dreams.
Don't ever give up.

You define you
No one else can tell you who you are.

Be strong

Ask God to guide you
and He will do it.

Interruption of My Schedule

I'm a regular person going about my retirement (but not really) days. Unforeseen by me, I have established a hectic schedule. No on purpose, mind you. At least I don't think so.

Well, I'm writing, volunteering, running a publishing company. I'm long on dreams, vision, energy. But really short on funds. So, add to this schedule the stress of trying to find the funds to pay for it.

Oh yes, I can pay my share of household bills with my "good government" retirement check. At least until heating, electricity and food costs started climbing. I still do make out fine. I simply can't do some things I used to do. What were those? Unimportant. Suffice it to say that I am okay with what I had to cut out.

I just need to get back to my level of tithing I'm accustomed to. Supporting my church is very important to me and I have not been as supportive, monetarily, lately. Oh I still volunteer my time so I give physical support. I teach Sunday School and sing in a choir. Blah, blah, blah... Well, I also added exercise into my busy schedule. I was walking regularly and going to a local fitness center to Zumba once or twice a week.

So as you can see, life's really not bad for me. I'm doing fine. Doing my thing and still keeping the house clean, I think. I also still prepare breakfast, lunch, snack and a pretty good dinner daily. Sounds like a super person right?

It sounds like a crazy person or simply workaholic as I've sometimes been called.

Looking at my schedule, you might ask, where's the fun. Writing is fun for me. Well until I became a professional and published author.

Zumba was fun until I stopped suddenly. Why did I stop? I had sort of an interruption of my schedule. I said "my schedule" so maybe it wasn't God's schedule.

Where shall I start? How about right here.

Now what's this cancer thing?

Yes, the "C" word. Actually the big "C" word.
I got my phone call as many others have before me, and many others will after.

Wow, what a shocker. A doctor calls to give me test results. You probably know this story. It's not so unusual. I had my annual mammogram. I received a call from a doctor indicating that something was found and that more tests were necessary. Well two biopsies later, I'm awaiting the results.

Good doctors go above and beyond what's okay to reach you to give you troubling test results. I know this because a long time ago, I received a call from a doctor on a Sunday afternoon. This time, the doctor called me multiple times; leaving messages on our home phone and my cell. We were out of town enjoying a brief break. As soon as I could, I called back.

Then I got the word.
Doctor's don't necessarily say they found something that may be cancer or cancerous over the phone. Maybe they think we will pass out or do something really stupid. This one said something like "according to the test results we found "_____" fill in the blank with the name of the type of cancer.

Then there was this pause as I digested the information. Then I asked the obvious question. What does that mean? Then another pause, then the doctor got pretty close to the "C" word like carcinoma _____ something or other. Think about it. This conversation can't be fun for the doctor either, at least a good and caring doctor.

Anyway, let me continue.

Another pause as I think some more. Then I say "Carcinoma sounds like cancer." The doctor indicates that that sounds about right.

Another pause as I try to think of something to say. Finally it comes.
"Well Dr. _____, what's next?" Then the real conversation began.

What's next? I receive a list of recommendations for doctors and cancer centers that accept my insurance.

Thank God for insurance even though it is expensive. My list would have been pretty empty without it. I probably would not have had the mammogram and two biopsies that found the cancer without it.

I pick a hospital that my husband and I like and their cancer center, and I make the call. I got my first appointment then I'm on my way. To what, I didn't really know.

But I need movement to something. Hopefully getting this stuff out of my body!

First appointment went extraordinarily well. Staff was polite and supportive. Doctor was friendly and listened to me and answered my questions in a way that I could understand. What more could I ask for? How about erasing this cancer thing from my body? Not happening.

We set the plan and schedule. The tests began. Another mammogram followed by another biopsy. Okay, I just had two about two weeks ago. Another one?

But guess what? Testing does not end easily. Some interesting results came from my third biopsy. Yep, had to have another one; an MRI biopsy. This was just in case there was no more cancer than they first thought. By this time, I am sick of biopsies. But wait, I do still have appropriate health insurance to have an MRI biopsy. I should not complain too much. Although I am really tired and really, really sore about now.

Okay celebration moment. There was no more additional cancer than they first found. Whoop! Whoop!

I had the surgery as originally planned with radiation treatment directly on the spot where the cancer was found. No more radiation treatment was necessary. No chemotherapy was necessary. Good news right?
Yes, most definitely. Back to my schedule?

Not just yet.

I was not so easily going to get away from my cancer doctor. For the next five years, I am to take Arimidex (Anastrozole) and visit the cancer institute every 3 months for a check up to be sure the cancer does not return. My schedule is not my own just yet.

Inside I am kicking and screaming like a spoiled child. They got everything right? Why do I need to continue to see a cancer doctor in a cancer institute? I'm healed right?My radiation doctor has an excellent sense of humor. He was not so humorous (serious face) as he explained to me why I needed to go through this 5-year process. He wanted to make sure he did not see me again under worse circumstances. Since he usually smiled a lot but not this time, I got the message.

Now back to my busy schedule. Not yet. Researching things that I am not supposed to eat. Changing my diet. No small task. It's a few months later and I still haven't gotten back to my schedule. Lots of crazy stuff going on in the world. I can't get to busy again. I need to be involved somehow.

Yes, I asked God many times why he allowed me to have this cancer thing. I'm still waiting for His answer. Right now I'm thinking that maybe it was to interrupt my busy schedule.

"And we know that all things work together for good to those who love God, to those who are the called according to His purpose." Romans 8:28 New King James Version (NKJV)

About the Author

As a creative writer (both traditional and innovative), Deborah Johnson is a proven senior professional with integrity and a high work ethic. She has provided and will continue to provide a fresh perspective with a sound foundation in all her endeavors. A researcher, writer and speaker, Ms. Johnson has a love of the written word. Deborah Johnson writes poetry and prose and enjoys writing opinion pieces on issues of the day.